Architecture Experience and Thought:
Projects by Tony Fretton Architects

Authors: Mark Cousins, Kenneth Frampton, Tony Fretton

AA Publications are initiated by the Chairman of the
Architectural Association, Mohsen Mostafavi.

Architecture Experience and Thought has been
produced to accompany an exhibition held at the
Architectural Association in London from 28 September
to 31 October 1998. AA exhibitions organizer:
Andrew Mackenzie.

The publication has been edited by Pamela Johnston
and designed by SMITH. Editorial assistants: Clare
Barrett, Sarah Dyson and Marilyn Sparrow.

ISBN 1 870890 93 0

ARCHITECTURE,
EXPERIENCE AND
THOUGHT

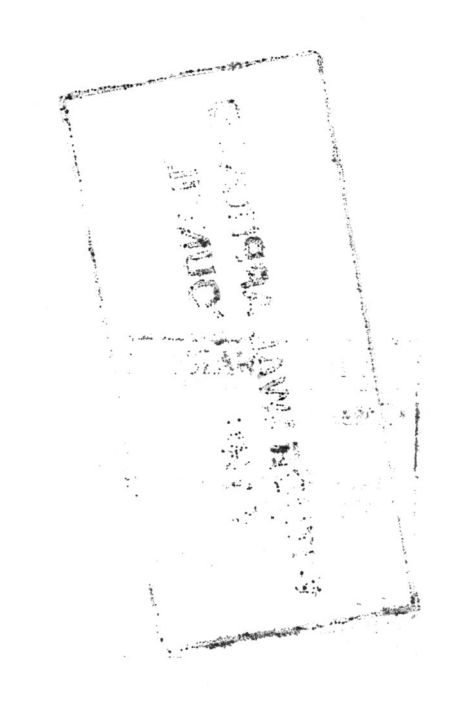

POETRY MAKES
NOTHING
HAPPEN

I COULD LIST THE THEMES IN THESE PROJECTS, OR ATTEMPT TO.

I COULD SAY, FOR EXAMPLE, THAT WE IDENTIFY A SOCIAL BACKGROUND BY NOTICING

THINGS AND DRAW THEM TO PEOPLE'S ATTENTION THROUGH WHAT WE DO WITH

THE BUILDING.

OR THAT THE POLITICS IN THE BUILDINGS AND OBJECTS THAT WE MAKE ARE LIBERTARIAN.

OR THAT APPEARANCE IS IMPORTANT FOR COMMUNICATING WITH THE PEOPLE THAT WE CAN

ONLY GUESS WILL USE THE BUILDINGS. OR THAT WE LOOK FOR EVERY OPPORTUNITY IN

THE PROGRAMME, LOCATION AND FORM OF THE BUILDING TO MAKE A BELIEVABLE PLACE.

OR THAT AT CERTAIN POINTS WHEN WE ARE DESIGNING, THE FORMS AND DETAILS OF THE

BUILDING START TO SAY THINGS DIRECTLY ABOUT THIS MOMENT IN TIME.

OR THAT IMAGES CAN BE AFFECTING AND THAT I REMEMBER SEEING PAINTINGS AND

BUILDINGS WHICH SPOKE DIRECTLY TO ME BEFORE I UNDERSTOOD THEM.

OR THAT I DESIGN FIRST, EXPERIENCE WHAT HAS BEEN DONE, AND THEN DRAW

CONCLUSIONS – ARCHITECTURE EXPERIENCE AND THOUGHT.

I COULD CONTINUE BUT I THINK THAT ARCHITECTURE,

OR ANY OTHER WORK OF CREATIVE PRACTICE, DOES NOT

COMMUNICATE IN ISOLATED EXPLANATIONS, AND THAT

THE DESCRIPTIONS OF THE PROJECTS AS OUT-BURSTS

OF RELATED FACTORS GET SLIGHTLY CLOSER.

BUILDINGS ARE ONE GREAT AREA WHERE THE

MUTUALITY AND INTERDEPENDENCE WHICH EXIST AT

THE ROOT OF SOCIETY CAN BE MADE VISIBLE AND

INSIGHTS ABOUT HOW WE MIGHT COME TO TERMS

WITH THE PRESENT CAN BE OFFERED THROUGH THE

POWER OF CREATIVITY, AS SUGGESTED IN W H AUDEN'S

BRILLIANT UNTRUTH, 'POETRY MAKES NOTHING

HAPPEN....

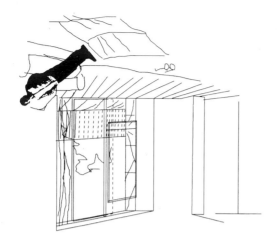

HOUSE IN LONDON

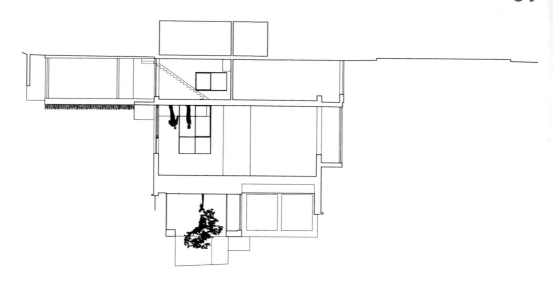

The site for this new house borders the grounds of Christopher Wren's Royal Hospital in Chelsea. The building is set back from the street and aligns with the house next to it to create a wider space at a curve in the road.

The house is entered either through a court, which is open to the sky and abundantly planted, or through the garage, which is designed as an interior room. Either route leads to a two-storey hall which has views into both the entrance court and the garden behind the house, giving an immediate sense of being within nature. The informal living room and kitchen face onto the garden and the formal dining room projects into it, separated from the garden walls by narrow courts filled with bamboo. The roof of the dining room is planted with tall grass and flowers, and the ceiling is frescoed.

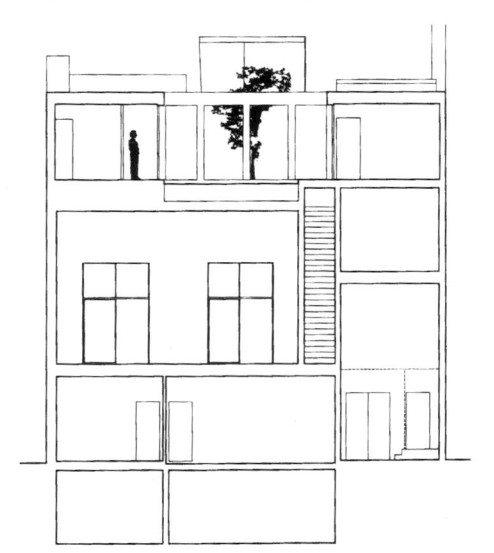

The garden is walled so that the only external view is of the trees in the Royal Hospital grounds, and is laid out sparsely, with plants and rocks around a single existing tree.

The garden can be seen from a balcony above. The first-floor lounge looks out over the balcony to the Royal Hospital; on the other side it looks through a bay window to the street. The room is high-ceilinged to provide a setting for paintings and sculpture; views and incidents in the plan create intimate locations within its large space. The balcony and the grass and flowers on top of the dining room occupy the foreground view from the rear windows; the long view is of the trees and spaces of the Royal Hospital grounds. The front bay window looks towards another nearby park, the Chelsea Physic Garden, and has an oblique view towards the river, over the entrance court.

By the side of the lounge is a small sitting room and concealed above it is a study that extends through the depth of the house. The enclosure of the trees and the projecting wall of the neighbouring house give the views from the study and sitting room an intimate scale.

The main stair is arranged as a formal flight from the entrance hall to the lounge, from where two concealed flights lead to the study and onto the roof, providing a momentary upward glimpse of sky from the doorway of the lounge.

The bedrooms are housed in two parallel pavilions placed on the roof either side of a tropical hothouse and a planted court. Nature is felt to be present throughout the house, stimulating the ornament and colour in the interior and the sensuousness of the exterior material of red sawn limestone.

Formal themes are established in the building and then adjusted in relation to location. The rooms are designed to invite use without fixing their purpose, to capture the unexpected beauty that exists in chance relationships and non-aesthetic arrangements.

Buildings which have preoccupied me have a presence in this work: the palace at Urbino, Dutch and Flemish houses where the windows exceed the area of the masonry, Le Corbusier's Maison Clarté in Geneva, Palladio's Villa Malcontenta and many buildings by Alvaro Siza and other architects who are working now. For me the architecture of the past and present exists in the present, always revealing its radicalness and capacity to talk about the heart of human experience.

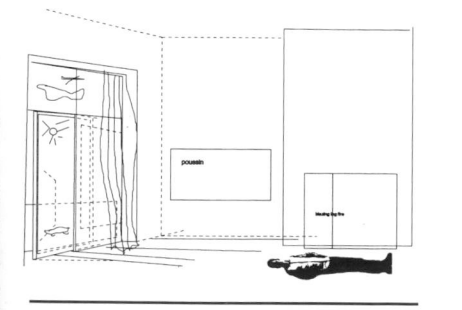

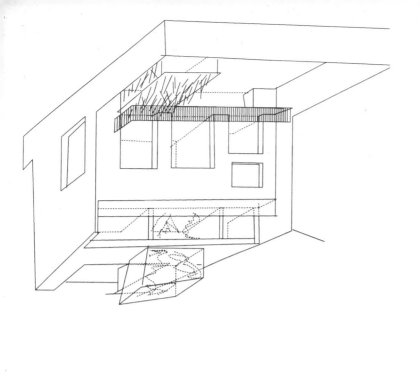

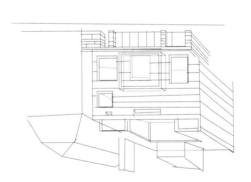

14

Basement

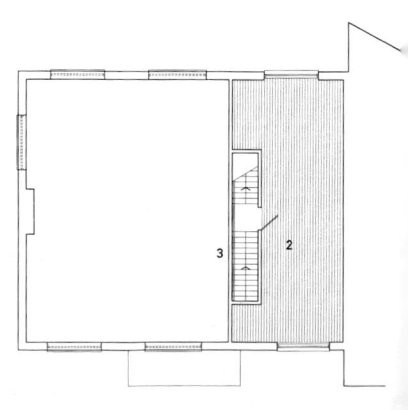

Second floor

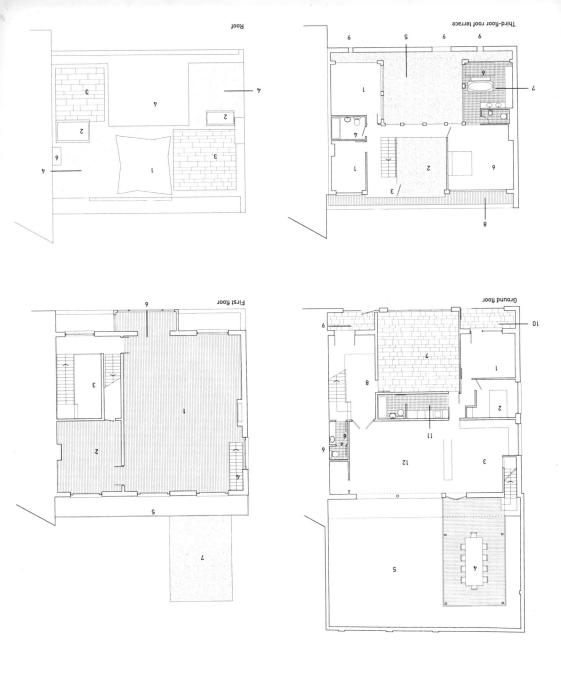

Roof

First floor

Third-floor roof terrace

Ground floor

CENTRE FOR VISUAL ARTS

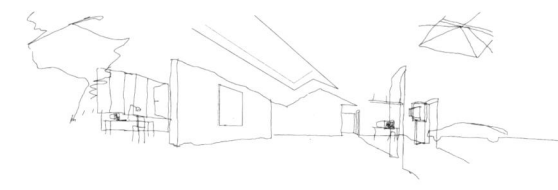

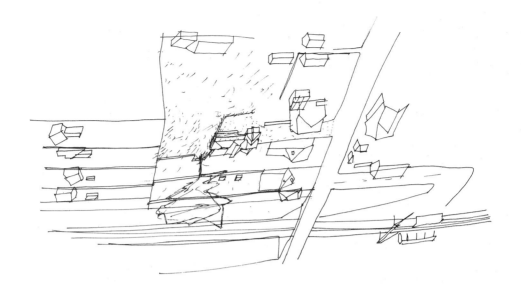

The Centre is in a field at the back of a long inclined gravel car park which changes to a field behind and looks onto some utilitarian buildings at the back of the main street: a doctor's surgery, builder's shed and telephone exchange.

The new building is excavated into the field so that it appears to be of the same scale as the original building attached to it. An entrance court is cut into the rising ground which leads to its principal room: an exhibition gallery with a rooflight along the length of its angled roof. At the side there is another gallery with a pyramidal roof cut off at an angle to form a rooflight. The original building houses a third gallery in which the ceiling has been opened up and the incline of the roof lined with cedar. The light in each gallery is of a different character; and can be progressively adjusted down to darkness. From the central gallery there are views into two teaching studios and, through them, to the village and field beyond.

For rapid construction, good thermal insulation and minimal maintenance, the building was made in timber framing and covered with unpainted boarding. The style of the building looks familiar but is invented.

One of the buildings on the other side of the site was converted into studios. The building was not elaborate and we worked within its range, adding a few elements. A new porch provides covered external circulation between the common room and the studios and makes the building resemble the new structure across the field. The existing window openings were cut down and filled with doors which open for access and views. The corrugated roof was renewed on the north side and extended over the porch; rooflights were installed over the studios. The original windows — into which sunlight filters through a tall hedge — were allowed to determine the planning.

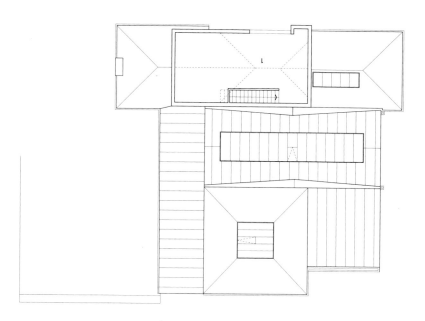

First floor

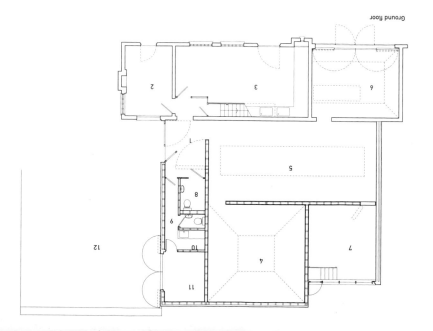

Ground floor

First floor
1 Offices

12 Entrance court
11 Store
10 Kitchen
9 Staff WC
8 Disabled WC
7 Studio 1
6 Gallery 3
5 Gallery 2
4 Gallery 1
3 Studio 2
2 Reception
1 Entrance
Ground floor

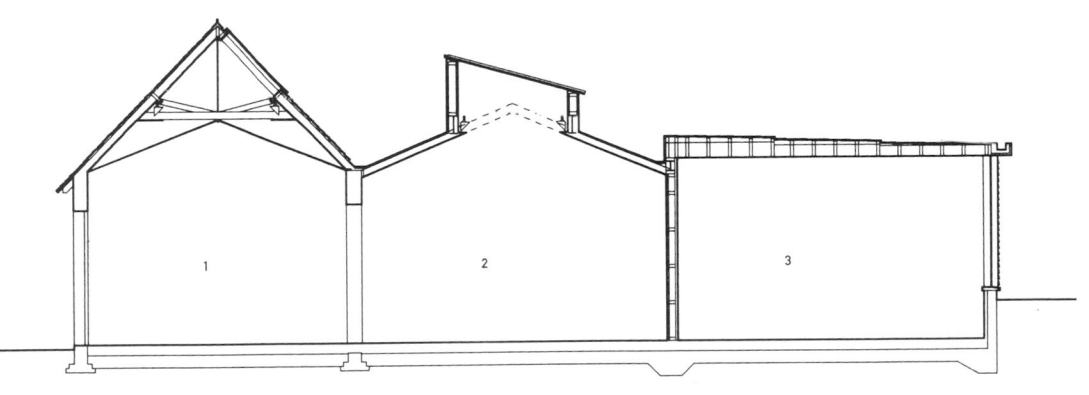

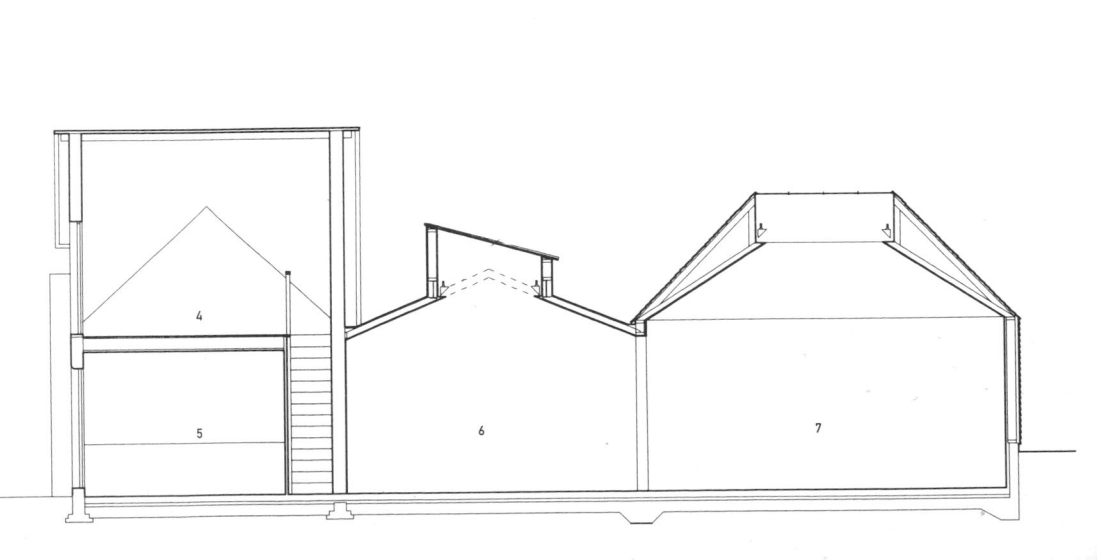

Studio building

1 Artist's Studio
2 Common Room
3 Kitchenette
4 WC/Shower Room
5 External Covered Walkway

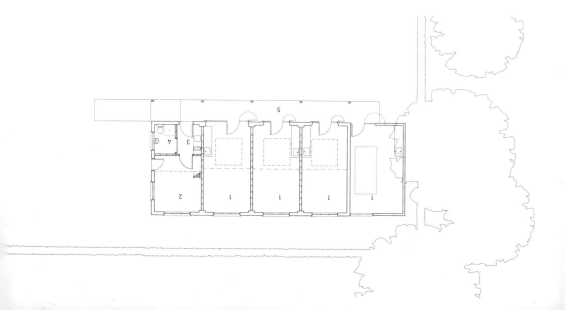

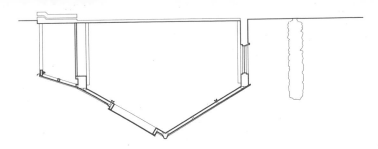

BRAD LOCHORE'S
HOUSE & STUDIO

Eighteenth-century London houses, like the later schemes of J J P Oud in Kiefhook, were frank and economic in their layout and construction and often romantically archetypical in expression. London houses were formally systematic yet could be adjusted to take advantage of particular circumstances. Oud's houses, although of the modern movement, were full of recognizable imagery: a garden shed seen through the back window, a traditional Dutch stairway.

The architecture of this project draws on these observations, and on bad buildings where beauty comes by chance, and on the desire to make the building a painted image of itself.

The building is an extension of a warehouse that is used as a house and studio, from which it grows in an unruly fashion, sitting on the studio as if backwards on a horse. The facades are of the same brick but lack architectural detail or modulation. Thinly and translucently painted, they are animated by the composition of the windows and doors and the activity in them.

The entrance door to the house is wide and furniture can be negotiated around the bend in the stair. The entrance to the studio is glazed and opens behind a mesh security screen to allow an interplay with the activities in the street.

The first floor is a living room that runs through the depth of the house. The kitchen and dining space look onto the street; mirrors on the window reveals increase the view. The other end contains the lounge, which looks onto a south-facing terrace and the banked-up rooflights of the studio.

Ground floor
1 Main studio
2 Shower room
3 WC
4 Office
5 Library
6 Entrance
7 Secondary stair
8 Utility

First floor
1 Living room
2 Existing loft
3 Terrace
4 Rooflights over studio

Second floor
1 Bedroom
2 WC/shower room
3 Existing loft
4 Terrace

Ground floor

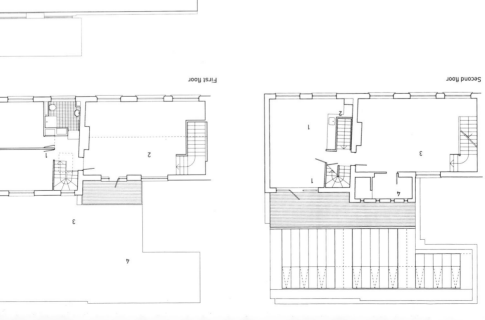

First floor

Second floor

CENTRE
QUAY ARTS

The Arts Centre occupies three industrial buildings facing the River Medina with a long secondary street running behind them. Two of the buildings connect at first-floor level across an inlet from the river; the third, originally a rope store with three very low storeys, is joined to the scheme by a new timber building. The boarded facade of this building continues the sinuous line of the back street and contains the back entrance, which is identified by the loading door placed above it. From the river side, the new building is a covered space which has a visual similarity to the volume of the slipway on the opposite bank. It is detailed as sparsely as a boat shed and relates in scale to the baulks used in a new terrace at the edge of the river.

In the mid-point of the sequence a stairway and a glass-sided lift lead to the theatre and exhibition space on the first floor. Here, a section of the roof crosses the river inlet in the open air to become a café surrounded by workshops.

The ground-floor space starts as the shop and box office in Sea Street, and ends in a gallery reached in the open air under the cover of the new building.

and columns was cut out and two of the roof pitches were joined to make the theatre area fully active for dance. The area can be arranged with 130 seats for theatre, music and film, with dressing rooms and a green room located in the rope store, or the seats can be retracted to create a space for classes and rehearsal. The exhibition space occupies the two arms of the remainder of the first floor. The space is artificially lit and has a single window for orientation, so lighting for exhibitions, especially those displaying film and video, can be accurately controlled.

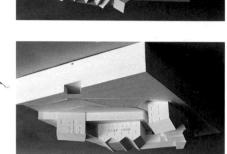

In this project the form of the building is the art form and the social form. The ground floor is a single public space, visible from the town, and the gallery and theatre, through their interiority, are a shared imaginary world.

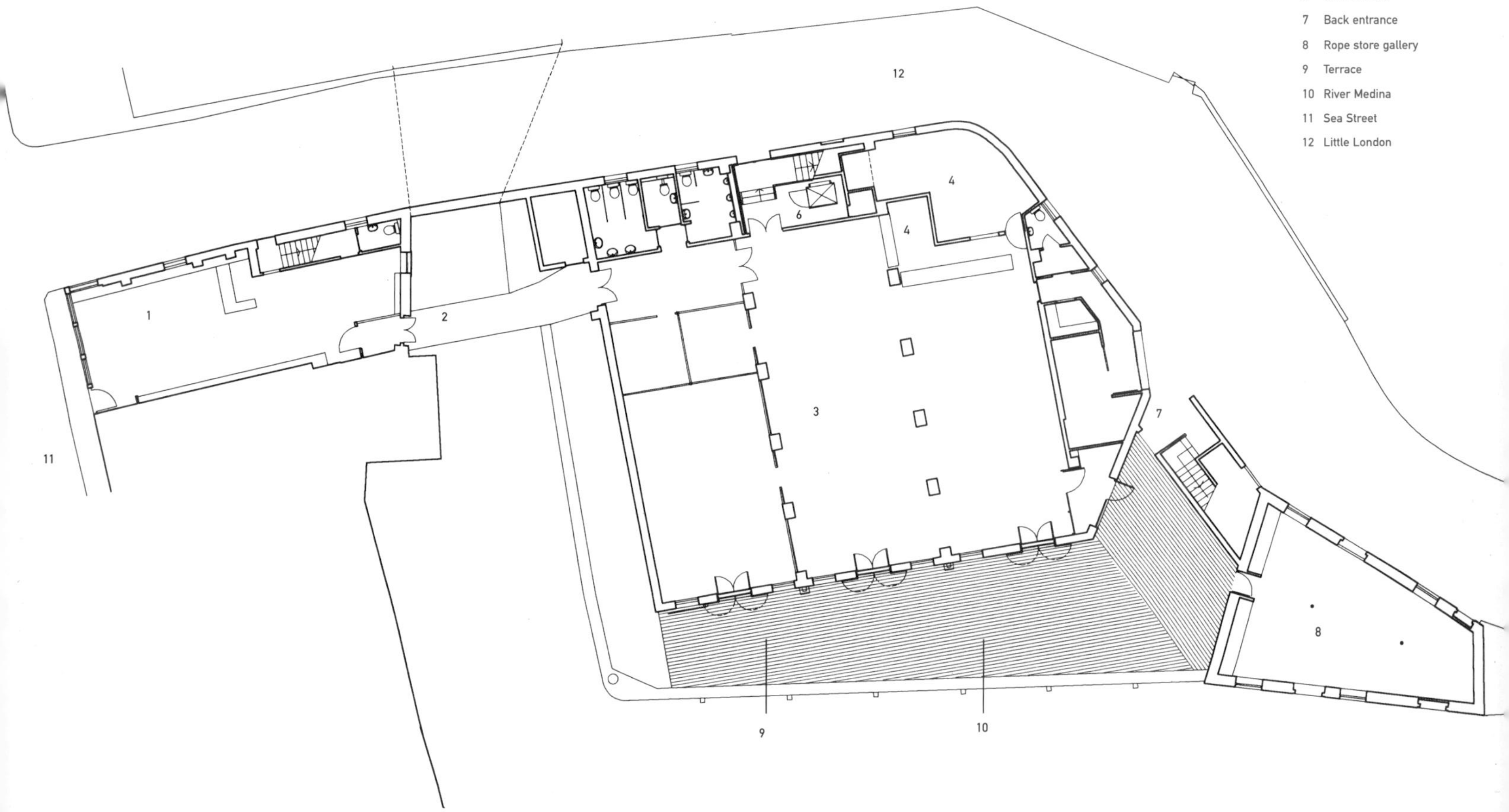

Ground floor
1   Shop
2   Bridge over Lukely Brook
3   Cafe and workshops
4   Kitchen
5   Bar
6   Stair and lift
7   Back entrance
8   Rope store gallery
9   Terrace
10 River Medina
11 Sea Street
12 Little London

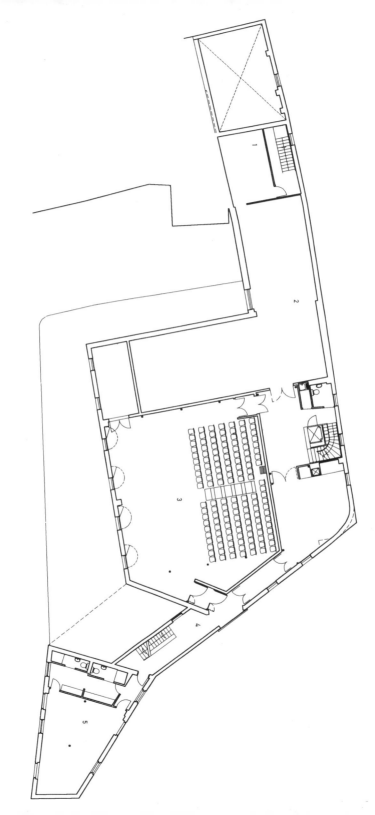

First floor

1 Video room
2 Gallery
3 Theatre space
4 Link
5 Changing and green room

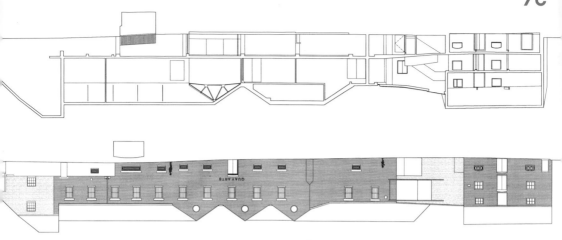

OPEN HAND
STUDIOS

The project will renovate the military tower which houses the studios of the artists' group, Open Hand, and add a gallery for an established programme of exhibitions and a studio for visiting artists. The site is on the edge of Reading but in the centre of an invisible network of activity, as the artists teach and exhibit in widely dispersed venues. This is only a design waiting, interminably, for financial approval, but I know it would make particular sense of this network, the emptiness of the adjoining military barracks and housing around it, and the highway with its remnants of a rural origin.

The gallery is proposed as a structure which has little presence in its external form yet is enclosing as an interior. The ceiling is of louvres, so the lighting track and daylight will be visible from some angles. One side of the gallery is glazed and screened off from the space to allow some of the exhibits to be seen from the highway.

The buildings are denied any effects of mass. Their walls are either transparent or resemble court walls with coverings of horizontal timber of the same pitch as brickwork, giving them the quality of walls found in Istanbul or English Georgian towns where brick architecture is transferred into timber construction. In a similar way the plan of the new gallery mimics that of the interior of the existing tower, the one being made of almost nothing, the other of visibly solid masonry. The visiting artists' studio is self-enclosed and hermetic with a top-lit studio and kitchen and its own external court.

These light and detail-less structures fill the space of the grounds and overcome the colossal insignificance of the existing building.

Ground floor

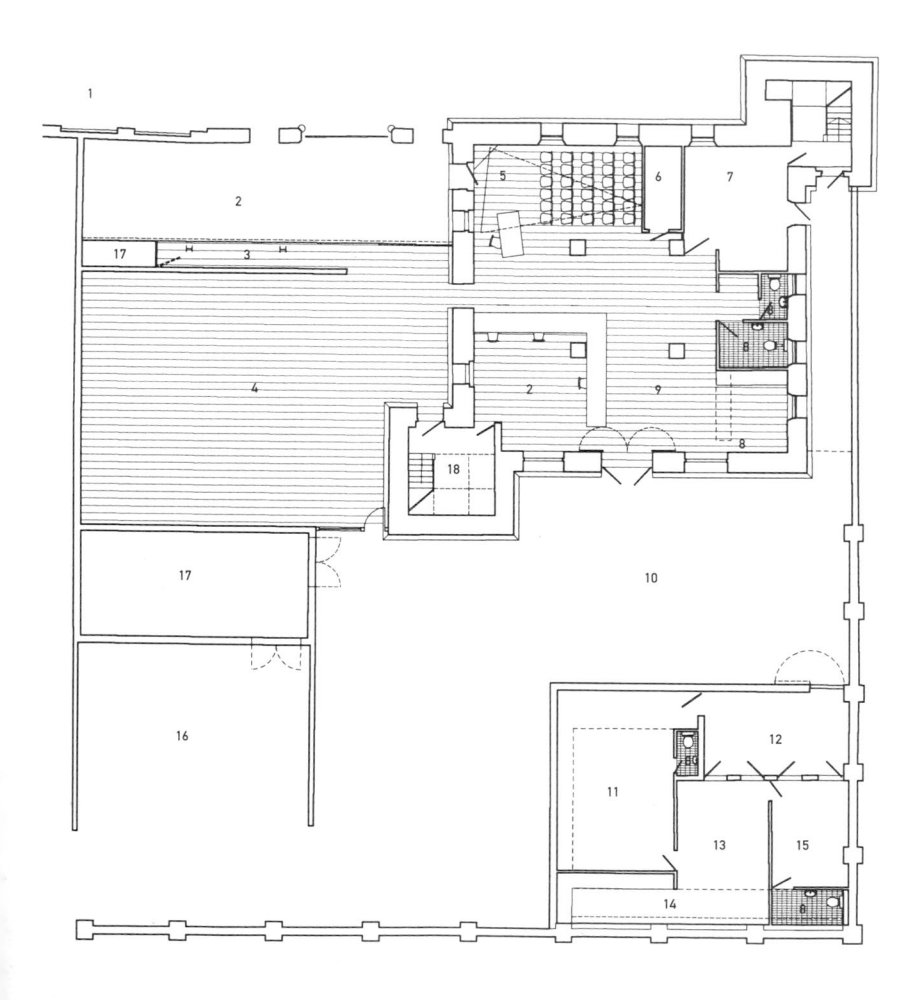

40

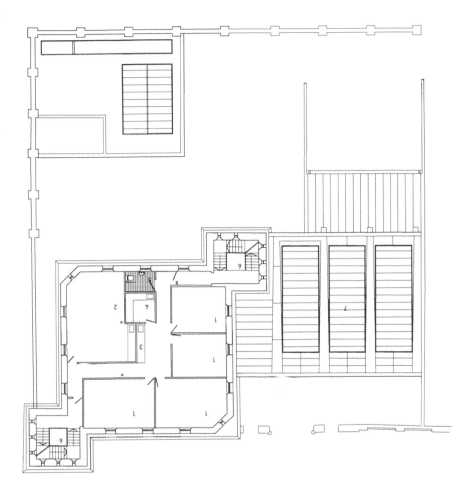

First and second floors

1 Resident artists' studio
2 Artists' common room
3 Sinks
4 Darkroom
5 WC
6 Stairwell
7 Gallery

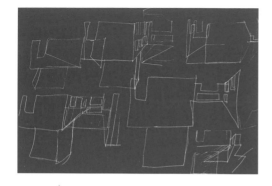

DANCE
FOR
CENTRE
LABAN

The character of the site is formed by the low scattered buildings which surround it, the water and form of Deptford Creek, and the extensive and open sky. The scheme asks how an institution in a remote location can be made a believable place.

The building that we proposed is a single form that extends over the whole site, drawing back from the boundaries to make open spaces, and turning inwards to form an entrance court and a garden court around which the school is organized. The entrance court is placed in a significant position, identified by the theatre fly-tower, and is lined with domestic-scale windows through which the activities of the theatre backstage and the school administration can be seen. On the north side is a walled car park which at one point looks into the interior garden. Along the east boundary the garden court lights the studios, whose windows are adjusted to give views of the Creek. From the west boundary a new path leads to the Creek, part of a series of informal spaces in the neighbourhood that include the nature park opposite the site and the grounds of the church in the distance. The roof of the building is planted with vegetation related to that in the Creek, nature park and garden court, so that other life forms are present in the scheme.

The two courts articulate the entrance foyer, café and theatre bar, giving each a distinctive character. The placing of these functions, with the reception desk and studio doubling as a practice stage and experimental theatre, crowds the space with activity.

Leading from this area to the school, a corridor provides places next to the garden court in which to stretch and relax. Further along its length seminar rooms, visiting artists' studios and other academic rooms are interspersed with dance studios so that people can meet. There are three stairways, animated by the activities taking place near them.

The upper floor is quiet and academic, containing the library, tutors' rooms and offices.

At key points there are views which locate the school in the wider locale. The character of the dance studios relates to their location. In the studio next to the car park a window above head height illuminates the dancers facing the mirror and gives a frontal orientation, as in a theatre. In other studios the windows give the dance floor equality in all directions, making them particularly suitable for contemporary dance.

The theatre is specifically designed for dance and brings the audience, principally of students and other dancers, close to the stage. The scenery store is located behind the stage where it doubles as a practice stage or opens up to make a deep performance area. The green room has a balcony which looks onto the Creek, and the control room can also open onto the Creek during setting up and practical training sessions in theatre lighting and sound.

The ideas of the construction are implicit in the design. The theatre and studios are naturally ventilated through a system of acoustically absorbent ducts and chimneys. Air is diffused into the studios through perforated wall panelling which conceals additional acoustic absorbants to keep speech intelligible.

The facades are configured as windows in a solid wall, providing measured enclosure and privacy, and controlling interior heat and illumination through the even distribution of daylight sources and reflective surfaces.

This format can retain its image while gaining life as it is adjusted during the development of the brief. Specific incidents such as canopies and balconies relate in scale to the nearby church and the surrounding industrial architecture. The exterior form establishes a concrete sense of location and mutuality with the surrounding area and provides an indicator of how it can change, while the sense of being in the wider world of dance occurs in the eye of the individual within the space.

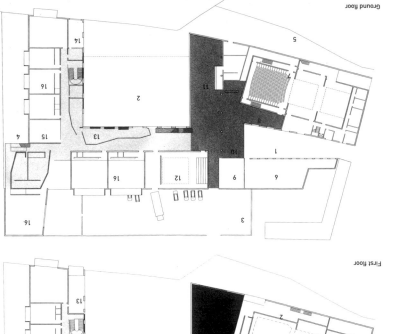

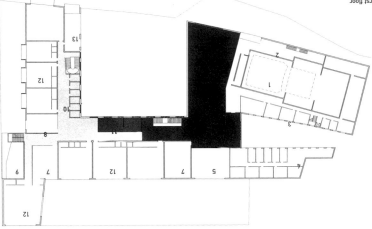

First floor

Ground floor

1 Entrance court
2 Garden
3 Car park
4 East court
5 Path to Creek
6 Sports injury clinic
7 Theatre
8 Theatre foyer
9 School office
10 Entrance hall/exhibition space
11 Café
12 Studio/practice stage/
experimental theatre
13 Dressing rooms
14 Students' common room
15 Visiting artists' studio
16 Dance studios

First floor

1 Theatre
2 Green room
3 Dressing and backstage rooms
4 Administration
5 Theatre design studio
6 Library
7 Seminar room
8 Visiting artists' studio
9 Dressing room
10 Tutors' rooms
11 Offices of Dance Theatre Journal
12 Dance studies
13 Faculty common room

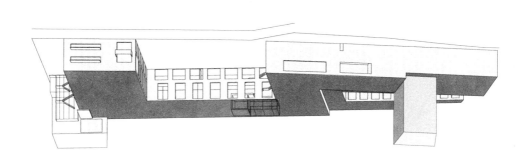

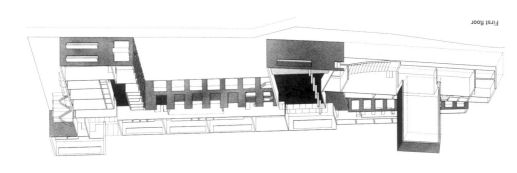

First floor

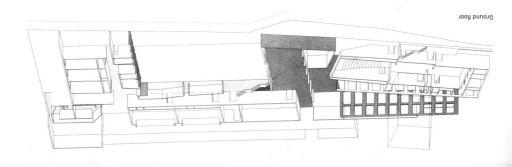

Ground floor

Conceptualism in art emerged some twenty-five years ago as a response to the crisis posed by the collapse of the modern project in the avant-gardist sense, in that modern art in either its figurative or abstract mode could no longer enjoy the impact it once had during the so-called heroic era between the two world wars. But what would become the fate of art in the latter part of this century had befallen architecture much earlier, with the idea of an 'architecture degree zero' that was first formulated by Adolf Loos circa 1908/1910 – a concept that ironically both inspired and undermined the Purist project of Le Corbusier. This drive to cut back the craft of architecture to its disjunctive origins somewhere between the lost vernacular of a Gothic past and the lost Doric of a classical age can be distantly felt in the work of Tony Fretton, to the extent that his practice seems to be predicated on the placing of a minimal structure within the confines of a carefully delineated site.

Nothing suggests this intent more forcibly than Fretton's initial sketches which seem to feel out the essence of a site, in order to inlay within its grain a simple cube or a bent shell. At the same time, these minimal gestures sometimes embody an abrasive materiality such as we find in Loos's townhouse for Tristan Tzara (1925), Alison and Peter Smithson's Soho House project (1952), or the ruined walls of Alvaro Siza's São Victor housing in Oporto (1974). Even these comparisons fall short of the grainy otherness of Fretton's vision, hovering somewhere between l'art brut and the sparse, aesthetic contrivance, say, of Robert Wilson's 1977 piece entitled 'I Was Sitting on My Patio, This Guy Came In, I Thought I Was Hallucinating'.

There always seems to be latent in Fretton's work some provocative sense of street art which is inimical to architecture, since by definition it is subversive, dramatic and provisional. One switches off the projector and the show is over – 'Nothing here, nothing there; a piece of string becomes an umbrella', as Pep Llinas put in it a totally different context, writing about the work of Alejandro de la Sota.

Despite this strong feeling for the immaterial, Fretton is prompt to insist that architecture includes the site with all its traces, that these endure across long periods of time and that this durability has a decisive impact on the ultimate character of the work. Perhaps this accounts for Fretton's economic-cum-topographic reading of the various sites where he has been asked to work, which is essential to his output to date as his penchant for cryptic aerial sketches or translucent close-ups.

Above: Buddhist Retreat, Holy Island.

Thus, he pictures Holy Island in terms of the ferry to the Isle of Arran from whence,

> if the weather and tide permit, a small boat will take you across... there is nothing on this island except small buildings and the faint remains of Celtic civilisation... with a thin layer of earth covering.

Similarly he describes the Walsall Art Gallery competition:

> Walsall is in Central England north of Birmingham, on the same latitude as Dublin and Hamburg and as far from London as Amsterdam is from Antwerp. The town's industry suffered in the recession of the 1980s, and it looked for financial recovery by redeveloping the centre as shopping malls. Though successful, they have made the centre lifeless, and more seriously, they prejudice civic freedom with the presence of private security guards who suppress any activity they feel is inappropriate.

The intentions lying behind his brilliant entry for the Laban Dance Centre are also detailed by the site:

> The character of the site is formed by the low scattered buildings which surround it, the water and form of Deptford Creek, and the extensive and open sky. The scheme asks how an institution in a remote location can be made a believable place. The building that we proposed is a single form that extends over the whole site, drawing back from the boundaries to make open spaces, and turning inwards to form an entrance court and a garden court around which the school is organized. The building has a green roof with vegetation related to that in the Creek, nature park and the garden court, so that other life forms are present in the scheme.

Despite his suggestive sketches and the precise indications of his critical intentions in the text, we are rarely provided with unequivocal and complete information as to either the limits of the site or the specifics of the solution. This laconic, all but evasive posture extends into the plans themselves, although here orthographic convention is such as to display the contrapuntal character of Fretton's volumetric inventions, particularly as evidenced in his proposals for the Walsall Art Gallery and the Laban Centre. In both instances and to different ends, a cultural programme is interpreted as an occasion to conjure up a 'city-in-miniature' with which to establish some kind of social-condenser for the surrounding neighbourhood. As Fretton describes his Walsall project:

> At work in the scheme is a recognition that collective structures exist in society, must exist simply in order that it can function, [these] are commonly revealed in the building's space and the ideas we share. Although the illusions of consumerism and individuality may mask them, their deep capability to offer cohesion, kindness and well-being, again and again remain unaltered.

Meanwhile, more than any other work by Fretton, the Laban Centre speaks of the body and its consummation through corporeal movement in space (see Tadao Ando's concept of *shintai* in relation to architecture). Thus, it is to be greatly regretted that this project did not prevail in the competition since this was surely his most convincing work to date. One has the sense that his laconic vision has, at times, proved hard to assimilate, partly due to the rigorous aesthetic adopted, but also due to an ethical, almost Puritan, refusal to go beyond the barest indications. Irrespective of whether the exhibit is a text or a drawing, terseness seems to prevail. Evidently this minimalist manner packs a punch of its own, but would it really be compromised by a more conventionally complete account?

One notes with relief that urban infill generally causes Fretton to focus more sharply on the precise constraints surrounding the work, as in the studio house for Brad Lochore or the art collector's house projected for an extremely promising site in Chelsea. This is an urban villa on a grand scale, of the kind that London has not seen since the days of Adam, and it will be ironic if it comes to be realized by an architect who is commonly regarded as an outsider. One hesitates to recognize these qualities lest the whole thing should turn into a mirage and yet here the house stands, as a project, within the grain of the street as it bends through the terraces that front onto the Chelsea Embankment. Confirmation is in the bay window of the *piano nobile* that provides oblique views of the river, and in the house's many other aristocratic features, including a double-height first floor devoted entirely to public reception with three 'classic' openings onto a balcony suspended above a courtyard garden. This balcony doubles as a belvedere from which to overlook the picturesque landscape of the Royal Hospital; at the same time, at grade, the house is treated as a virtual patio dwelling with a fully glazed dining pavilion projecting out into a walled court.

Thus shades of Mies van der Rohe one the one hand and of Le Corbusier (Maison Plainex) on the other, not to mention references to the ubiquitous Loos on the roof, where the master bedroom sequence gives rise to another courtyard garden. Without any literal allusions in terms of style, the tropes pile up none the less on the street front like a series of assimilated tracts. Thus, one is reminded of Loos's Steiner House or his Villa Moisi, of Auguste Perret's villa for Nubar Bey at Garches, while the coursed stonework suggests a source closer to our own time, most notably the work of de la Sota. Here we have grandeur with a capital G but also with restraint and modesty. Thus one comes to the end of the century and reads once again, 'Nothing here, nothing there, a piece of string...'.

Tony Fretton's work has attracted strong support from architects, clients and critics. In particular the Lisson Gallery is acknowledged as an exemplary space, both in its function as a gallery and in the complex relations it establishes with the site. Yet the published commentary on his work has a somewhat bemused character: the evident wish to praise seems to run into an invisible obstacle and

is often diverted into an identification of virtues. The buildings are described as 'subtle', 'responsive', even 'modest' – terms whose architectural meaning seems obscure. At the same time they are called 'disjunctive' and 'unsettling'. It is as if the critics are not sure what is being done, even if they are sure it is being done well. It feels as if the projects have missing pages: there is no evident stylistic or architectural signature to provide a critical point of reference.

But perhaps this is not the level at which to assess the coherence of the practice. This is not a practice which exists at the level of purely architectural dimensions. It is not one which fits into the current schools of architectural design – in a sense it could not, for reasons I hope will become clear. But it is a practice which has a wealth to teach about how architecture can make a complex contribution to the city and its capacity to be an emotional object of thought. For the purposes of this argument I will call this civil architecture.

The term itself is dangerously misleading, too easily associated with civic architecture – its exact opposite. Civic architecture usually entails the imposition of a social ideology upon the urban fabric. What I am calling civil architecture, by contrast, is an architecture which bridges two worlds through a gesture of inclusion, confronting the subject with an element at the intersection of a culture and the subject's perception. In this sense the very term *civil* has a strangeness about it which needs to be rediscovered: it can refer to peaceful intent, recognition, the use of conventional artifice, the city outside the relation to the state, a certain reserve, communicating without necessarily meaning. This scope can seem bizarre. What is it that yokes such apparently disparate elements into a single term? This can only be addressed through an even odder term – happiness. Happiness is not a category with an elevated history within modernism, which would tend to dismiss it as a state at variance with

Above: Lisson Gallery, London.

seriousness. (Anguish has played a much more significant role in artistic and architectural thought.) Yet there is something about the relation between buildings and people which is precisely concerned with happiness, and indeed with a relation to the civil.

The civil is the moment when the construction of culture is revealed to the subject as an immediate sensation; indeed that very sensation *is* the construction of culture. The civil involves a dialectic concerning complexity and simplicity. The artefact is complex — it is the memory of other buildings, the knowledge of building, the fundamental reworking of something — but it is simple in its offices. The subject who accepts the gesture experiences a happiness. He may even accept that the building has been pleased to see him. This 'happiness' is not a vague thing; it is not euphoria; it is even prior to aesthetic pleasure. In this it is like those dreams which, however implausible, leave us with an undeniable sense of reality when we wake: a complex experiment which reveals the ordinary, the ordinarily human. This question of 'happiness', then, is the moment when in the manifold of perception the subject apprehends that something is both made and real, but is not harmful. In this it touches the civil promise of architecture, a promise which is not frequently kept. Humans find themselves surrounded by objects which can seem both made and real but also harmful, or by made objects which lack reality. Tony Fretton acknowledges something of this: 'Solo performance made me hypersensitive to the relationships between humans and the material world. To explore this area, I frequently use ordinary everyday objects including established building types.' This is not phenomenology; it is an experimental performance. This performative quality is not about what the building 'means' or 'says' but is an attempt to construct the civil gesture.

This happiness is not only happiness; it is the condition for making a critique. Once accepted the gesture can be employed by the subject in the service of criticism. Fretton wrote of the Lisson Gallery that 'the elevation… rhymes with the surrounding high-rises, voids and objects to point out that these are not mistakes or by-products, but part of an unconscious project that has to be acknowledged… they shine a light on a continual process which requires more than architecture to happen'. William Mann commented: 'it follows from this that the most effective strategy for the architect is to incorporate this process into their work, using established conventions in order to destabilize them, rather than attempting to change them wholesale.'[1]

This civil gesture leads to an approach to architectural design which does not fit most critical

1 From William Mann's article in *Archis*, July 1995; 'Tony Frettons ontwriching van het alledaagse/Tony Fretton's Dislocation of the Everyday'.

categories. Of course, as with other practices of this size and independence, the series of projects reflects not so much the architect's choice but the history of commissions, and it would be absurd to define the practice in terms of the type of work undertaken. Yet there is a consistency which reflects the fundamental gesture and sets itself against a number of contemporary trends. Each new project derives from Fretton's elimination of its origin; wherever and however, he is always doing *another* building. This sense of *another* goes in two directions. Firstly it goes backwards, to the memory of other buildings, although this is anything but the existence of historical examples, still less a practice of quotation. Rather it bears on what has been said of Dan Graham: '[He] counters the historicist past with the conception of an actual though hidden past mostly eradicated from consciousness but briefly available in moments not obscured by the dominant ideology of the new.'[2] This has an unusual consequence: to the memory everything is vernacular by definition. William Mann described this as a recognition by Fretton:

> that it is possible to reclaim for architecture the very large territory represented by the vernacular, without the use of familiar proportions, motifs or tectonic language. He believes that the various spatial and material innovations are now assimilated into the field of accepted meanings; having lost their novelty they can now serve as part of an expanded vernacular. This has nothing to do with quotation or eclecticism but is rather an exploration of the resonance which shared meanings confer on our material culture.

The other direction of *another* building is in terms of the city. Whether or not the site is clear or involves the reworking of existing buildings is not a fundamental question for the civil gesture; it is *always* as much a response as it is an intervention. Again this is not, in current terms, a 'sensitivity to context', a modesty in respect to what is. It is a recognition that all building is rebuilding, that all gestures are constrained by being in a series. So-called originality can be the autism of architecture. An 'original' gesture could never be recognized: if it is recognized, it would have been awaited. It might be objected that the invocation of the city leaves out those projects which are if not in the country then outside the town. But the civil has priority here too. Nature itself, coded by memory, becomes itself the vernacular of the gesture. There is no attempt to represent Nature, or to mimic the organic. Nature, remembered, is of the hands which have shaped it. There is no external 'other' in this architecture.

In this it undercuts the pre-modernism that lurks in modernism. The myths of originality, of

2 See the introduction to Dan Graham, *Rock My Religion*, edited by B. Wallis (MIT Press).

creating *ex nihilo* the concept of a site – all these drew modernism back into a heroism of the original. Tony Fretton's practice uses modernism but it is one which is never pristine, is now disenchanted and can be freed for use. If this involves an ambivalence about modernism, it places him firmly outside the nonsense about post-modernism. There are different ways of trying to put this issue; one way is to note that there is a profound difference between the narratives of modernist architecture and modern art, especially in the way they are represented historically. Many accounts of twentieth-century architecture are still under the impression that there was an end to modernism and that for better or for worse something called post-modernism took its place, or filled the vacuum. This story is told in terms of a reaction at the *level of style*. As a consequence such histories regress the analysis of architecture into that of style and retreat into the same form of narratives which describe how the Renaissance became the Baroque. Art history has damaged architectural analysis by privileging this link between period and style. Accounts of the fate of modernist art practice are more thoughtful, and more related to the larger fate of modernism. They are concerned, not with the trivial question of the post-modern, but with what we might call the after-life of modernism, with the reworking of modernist art practice to fulfil other objectives as it is translated into other worlds. For it is a question of what happens when modernism is a given.

The historiography of modernist art is at its greatest difference from contemporary architectural practice in what has been called minimalism. It is indeed this critical distance which produces some of the critical stumbling over the work of Tony Fretton. For on occasion his work has been described as 'minimalist'. Nothing could be further from it. Minimalism in architecture bears no evident relation to the work of Judd, André and Flavin, and it is comic to see its proponents claim such an affinity. Most so-called minimalism is precisely a style, a currently fluent and commercially desirable surface. Confident that less is more, its proponents cannot even value the less, unless it is the less that makes more. In effect this minimalism is the designer *feng shui* of the commodification of the space of commodities. It reflects the scarcity of emptiness in a world where now it is the poor who are cluttered. This has little bearing on the concerns of artistic minimalism. Tony Fretton's work, which has no connection to current architectural minimalism, none the less does relate to the work of minimalist art. But it does so at the level of the object itself. The already made elements of that art – the issue of seriality, the geometries of a kind of social ubiquity – are aspects which penetrate the work as a resource. It has nothing to do with surfaces, but bears on the memory of modernity expressed in construction.

I have tried to argue that the strength and independence of Fretton's practice lie in its fundamental conformity to a civil gesture. Unfortunately the terrain of this argument is obscured by many humanist panegyrics to this or that architect on the basis of their humaneness, their sensitivity to culture and location, their aspiration for a better life, etc. Architectural writing is littered with these clichés. It would be better to imagine this civil gesture as being anti-humanist. It is founded not upon a utopianism or a general doctrine of emancipation, but upon an analysis of contemporary culture. This requires an instinct for working at that exact and exacting intersection where the signifying elements of a culture touch the affective life of the subject. For it is that place where complexity and a momentary happiness meet which constitutes, for better or for worse, the life of a culture. It was for this reason that Freud made the fundamental link between Eros and the building of cities.

The office of Tony Fretton Architects

Project Architects:
Jude Brown
Jim McKinney
Tom Russell
Deborah Saunt

Assistants:
Karl Karason
Ralph Blaettler
Hendrine den Hengst
Sophie Laenen
Glenn Lowcock
Natanho Nosigres
Myrka Wisniewski

Photo credits:
Ralph Blaettler 21 (left), 22 (above), 24–25
Lorenzo Elbaz 17–19, 21 (right), 22 (below)
Tony Fretton 21 (centre), 32 (below)
David Grandorge 31, 33 (below), 47
Glenn Lowcock 9, 13, 28, 38, 41
Morley von Sternberg 32 (above), 33 (above), 36, 37